MathFlare

Name: ______________________

Class: __________

Teacher: ______________________

Introduction

As parents and educators, we recognize the pivotal role mathematics plays in shaping a child's academic journey and future success. Yet, the path to mathematical proficiency can often seem daunting, fraught with challenges and complexities. That's where the transformative power of MathFlare Workbooks shine through, illuminating the way forward with clarity, precision, and purpose.

Introducing MathFlare Workbooks – a beacon of guidance, a testament to excellence, and a catalyst for achievement. Crafted with meticulous care and expertise, MathFlare Workbooks stand as paragons of educational excellence, designed to nurture young minds, ignite a passion for learning, and develop a deep-rooted understanding of mathematical concepts.

Picture this: your child eagerly delves into the pages of Mathflare Workbook, greeted by a step-by-step guide illuminated with vivid examples that demystify complex mathematical concepts. With each turn of the page, they embark on a journey of discovery, encountering thoughtfully curated practice questions that reinforce learning and hone problem-solving skills. And when they unveil the answers to those very questions, a sense of accomplishment blossoms within them – a tangible reward for their hard work and dedication.

But MathFlare Workbooks are more than just tools for learning; they are pathways to comprehension, fostering a deep-seated understanding of mathematical concepts through a sequential, logical flow. From fundamental principles to advanced problem-solving strategies, every chapter builds upon the last, ensuring a robust foundation upon which future knowledge can be constructed.

As parents, we yearn for nothing more than to see our children thrive, to witness the spark of inspiration ignited within them as they conquer academic challenges with confidence and poise. MathFlare Workbooks serve as partners in this noble endeavor, offering not just practice questions, but the keys to unlocking a world of opportunity.

And for teachers, MathFlare Workbooks stand as invaluable allies in the quest to cultivate mathematical proficiency in the classroom. With answers readily available, instructors can focus on guiding and nurturing their students, confident in the knowledge that MathFlare Workbooks provide a solid framework upon which to build.

In the pages of MathFlare Workbooks, we find not just the promise of academic excellence, but the seeds of a brighter tomorrow. So let us embrace the power of mathematics, let us champion the journey of learning, and let us pave the way for a generation of young minds poised to shape the world. With MathFlare Workbooks as our guide, the possibilities are infinite, and the future, bright.

Table of Contents

MathFlare
MATH WORKBOOK
5
Step by Step Guide and Essential Practice with Answers
Multiplication Division
Place Value and Expanded Notations
Fractions and Geometry
Unit Conversion
MathFlare Publishing

MathFlare
MATH WORKBOOK
5-6
Step by Step Guide and Essential Practice with Answers
Multiplication Division
Place Value and Expanded Notations
Fractions and Geometry
Units and Statistics
MathFlare Publishing

MathFlare
MATH WORKBOOK
6
Step by Step Guide and Essential Practice with Answers
Integers and Statistics
Arithmetic and Pre-Algebra
Fractions and Geometry
Ratio and Percentage
MathFlare Publishing

MathFlare
MATH WORKBOOK
6-7
Step by Step Guide and Essential Practice with Answers
Arithmetic and Pre-Algebra
Ratio, Percent Proportion
Geometry
Statistics
MathFlare Publishing

MathFlare
MATH WORKBOOK
7
Step by Step Guide and Essential Practice with Answers
Pre-Algebra
Ratio, Percent Proportion
Geometry
Statistics
MathFlare Publishing

MathFlare
MATH WORKBOOK
7-8
Step by Step Guide and Essential Practice with Answers
Pre-Algebra
Ratio, Percent Proportion
Geometry and Cartesian Plane
Statistics
MathFlare Publishing

MathFlare
MATH WORKBOOK
8-9
Step by Step Guide and Essential Practice with Answers
Pre-Algebra
Ratio, Proportion and Percentage
Linear Equations
Geometry and Cartesian Plane
MathFlare Publishing

MathFlare
MATH WORKBOOK
8
Step by Step Guide and Essential Practice with Answers
Pre-Algebra
Percentage
Linear Equations
Geometry
MathFlare Publishing

Place Value and Expanded Notations

Place value tells us the value of a digit in a number based on where it's placed.

Imagine we have the number 753. It has three digits: 7, 5, and 3.

Now, each digit holds a special place:

The digit 7 is in the hundreds place. It means it represents seven groups of 100.

The digit 5 is in the tens place. It means it's representing five groups of 10.

The digit 3 is in the ones place. It means it represents three single units.

So, when we want to know the total value of the number 753, we add up the values of each digit based on its place value:

The digit 7 in the hundreds place is worth 700.

The digit 5 in the tens place is worth 50.

The digit 3 in the ones place is worth 3.

When we add these values together, we find the value of the entire number:

700 + 50 + 3 = 753

Let's solve problems from the exercises:

Place value of the underlined digit:

125 = 1 hundred

Expanded notations:

260   2 hundreds + 6 tens

124   1 hundred + 2 tens + 4 ones

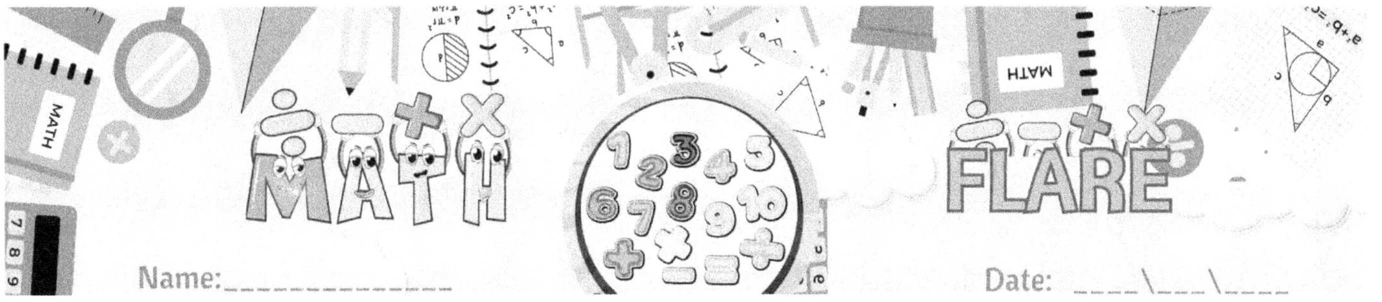

Name:______________________   Date: ___________

Place Value

Determine the place value of the underlined digit.

1. 4,347 = ____________________

2. 1,189 = ____________________

3. 846 = ____________________

4. 2,862 = ____________________

5. 2,120 = ____________________

6. 1,036 = ____________________

7. 6,921 = ____________________

8. 1,702 = ____________________

9. 7,101 = ____________________

10. 8,235 = ____________________

11. 195 = ____________________

12. 6,011 = ____________________

13. 90 = ____________________

14. 8,583 = ____________________

15. 868 = ___________________

16. 6,848 = ___________________

17. 1,523 = ___________________

18. 1,017 = ___________________

19. 3,262 = ___________________

20. 6,845 = ___________________

21. 6,545 = ___________________

22. 2,913 = ___________________

23. 7,626 = ___________________

24. 3,532 = ___________________

25. 6,353 = ___________________

26. 3,982 = ___________________

27. 9,359 = ___________________

28. 5,657 = ___________________

29. 8,607 = ___________________

30. 9,763 = ___________________

31. 4,748 = _______________

32. 7,644 = _______________

33. 3,752 = _______________

34. 3,428 = _______________

35. 5,308 = _______________

36. 677 = _______________

37. 8,637 = _______________

38. 552 = _______________

39. 5,064 = _______________

40. 3,230 = _______________

41. 1,163 = _______________

42. 7,133 = _______________

43. 7,904 = _______________

44. 6,777 = _______________

45. 14 = _______________

46. 496 = _______________

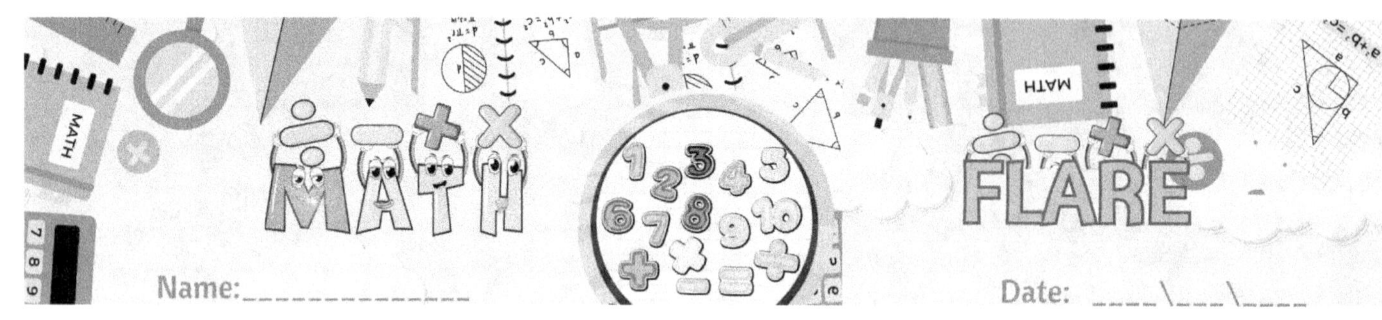

47. 3,7<u>4</u>8 = _________________

48. 8,3<u>3</u>5 = _________________

49. 4,<u>5</u>79 = _________________

50. 5,9<u>6</u>5 = _________________

51. 3,<u>5</u>94 = _________________

52. <u>5</u>,262 = _________________

53. 2,40<u>1</u> = _________________

54. 5,<u>5</u>44 = _________________

55. 4,0<u>5</u>2 = _________________

56. 1,<u>4</u>35 = _________________

57. 3,5<u>6</u>2 = _________________

58. 7,31<u>3</u> = _________________

59. <u>6</u>,508 = _________________

60. 8,13<u>7</u> = _________________

61. 1,67<u>6</u> = _________________

62. 1,26<u>5</u> = _________________

63. 3,095 = _______________________

64. 7,337 = _______________________

65. 3,487 = _______________________

66. 2,549 = _______________________

67. 2,259 = _______________________

68. 6,661 = _______________________

69. 3,276 = _______________________

70. 192 = _______________________

71. 8,210 = _______________________

72. 972 = _______________________

73. 5,952 = _______________________

74. 32 = _______________________

75. 5,683 = _______________________

76. 9,412 = _______________________

77. 5,008 = _______________________

78. 850 = _______________________

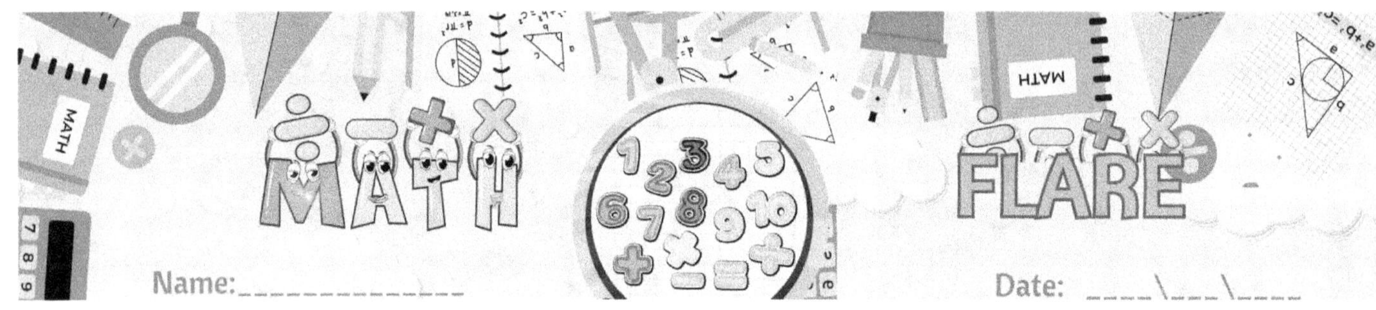

Date:

Place Value: Expanded Notation

Provide the expanded notation for each value.

79. ______________ 6 thousands + 2 hundreds + 7 tens + 3 ones

80. ______________ 7 thousands + 9 hundreds + 9 tens

81. ______________ 8 thousands + 5 hundreds + 1 ten + 6 ones

82. ______________ 2 thousands + 3 hundreds + 6 tens + 2 ones

83. ______________ 7 thousands + 9 hundreds + 4 tens + 5 ones

84. ______________ 7 hundreds + 7 tens + 3 ones

85. ______________ 2 thousands + 8 hundreds + 5 tens + 2 ones

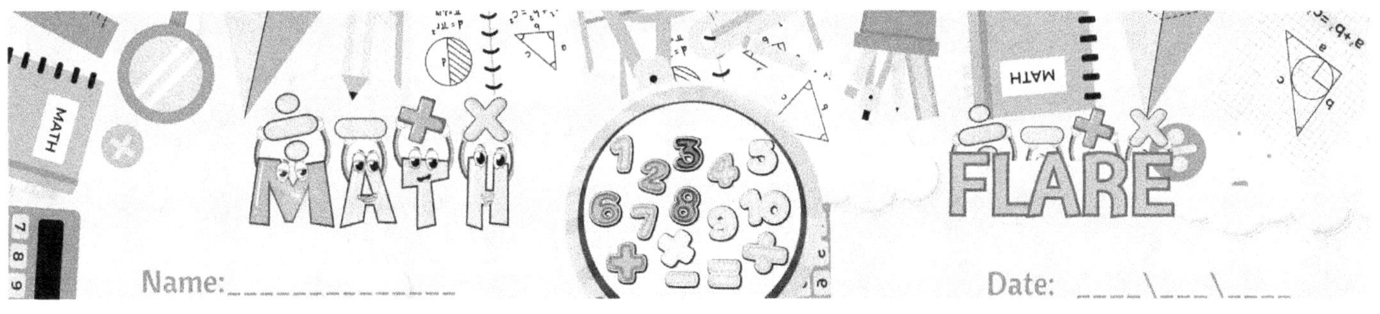

Name:_______________   Date: ____________

86. _______________ 1 thousand + 8 hundreds + 3 tens + 4 ones

87. _______________ 8 thousands + 9 tens + 5 ones

88. _______________ 6 thousands + 4 hundreds + 7 tens + 8 ones

89. _______________ 2 thousands + 1 ten + 6 ones

90. _______________ 1 thousand + 5 hundreds + 3 tens + 6 ones

91. _______________ 2 hundreds + 8 tens + 5 ones

92. _______________ 7 thousands + 5 tens + 3 ones

93. _______________ 1 hundred + 7 tens + 3 ones

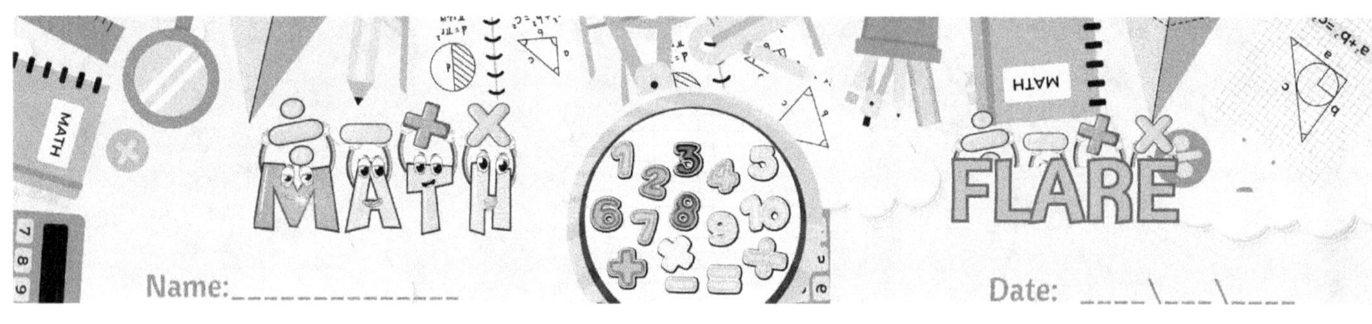

94. __________ 7 thousands + 2 hundreds + 1 ten + 1 one

95. __________ 3 thousands + 2 hundreds + 5 ones

96. __________ 1 thousand + 9 hundreds + 4 tens + 5 ones

97. __________ 8 thousands + 9 hundreds + 8 tens + 7 ones

98. __________ 4 thousands + 5 hundreds + 4 tens + 2 ones

99. __________ 4 thousands + 9 hundreds + 6 tens + 1 one

100. __________ 8 thousands + 1 hundred + 3 tens + 8 ones

101. __________ 3 thousands + 7 hundreds + 1 ten + 6 ones

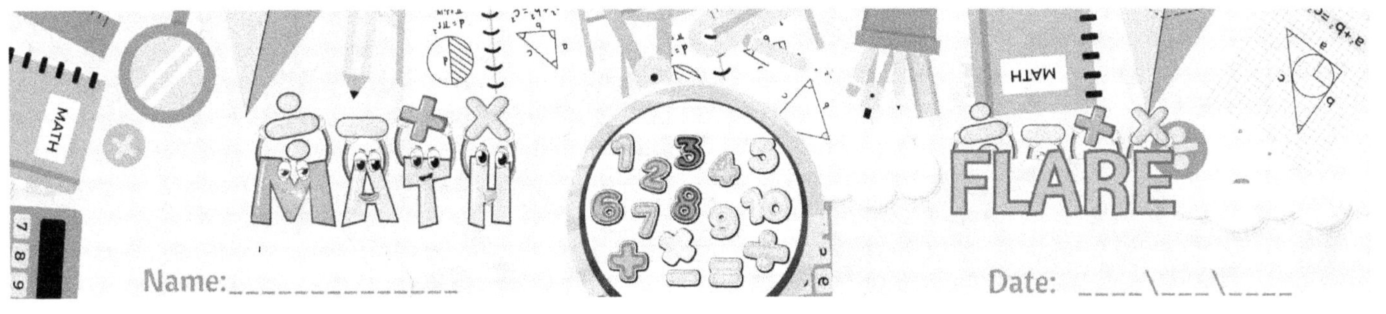

Name:_______________________ Date: ____________

102. ________________ 3 thousands + 6 hundreds + 8 tens + 4 ones

103. ________________ 4 thousands + 8 tens + 3 ones

104. ________________ 1 thousand + 6 hundreds + 8 tens + 1 one

105. ________________ 4 thousands + 6 hundreds + 4 tens

106. ________________ 5 thousands + 3 hundreds + 1 ten + 8 ones

107. ________________ 7 thousands + 7 hundreds + 8 tens + 2 ones

108. ________________ 5 thousands + 3 hundreds + 7 tens + 2 ones

109. ________________ 9 thousands + 3 tens + 5 ones

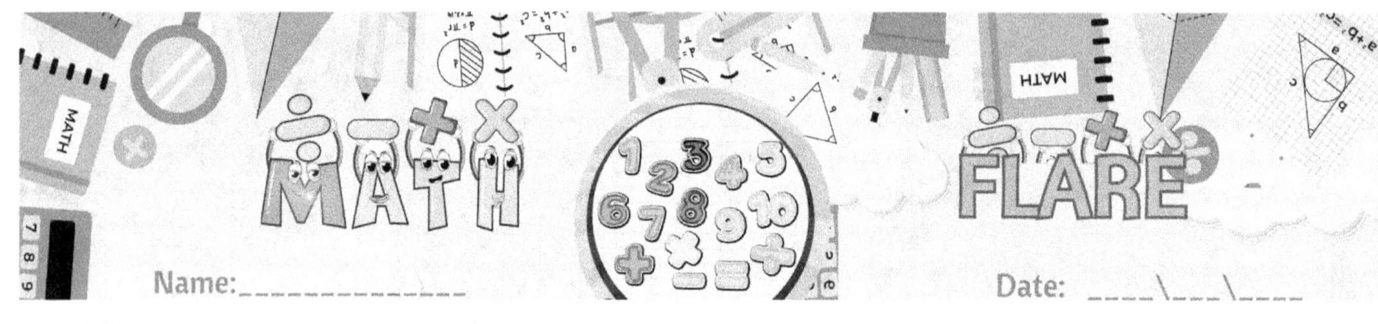

110. ________________ 4 thousands + 7 tens

111. ________________ 4 thousands + 3 hundreds + 2 tens

112. ________________ 2 thousands + 7 hundreds + 8 tens + 2 ones

113. ________________ 5 thousands + 1 hundred + 5 tens + 7 ones

114. ________________ 9 thousands + 8 tens + 8 ones

115. ________________ 7 thousands + 9 hundreds + 7 tens + 6 ones

116. ________________ 7 thousands + 6 tens + 8 ones

117. ________________ 1 thousand + 6 hundreds + 2 tens + 2 ones

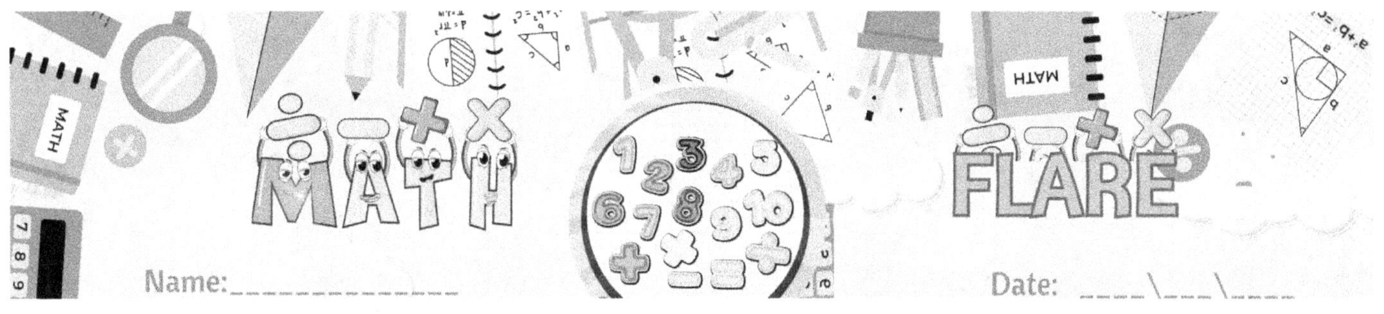

118. _______________ 2 thousands + 4 hundreds

119. _______________ 2 thousands + 8 hundreds + 8 tens + 8 ones

120. _______________ 9 thousands + 5 hundreds + 2 tens + 4 ones

121. _______________ 1 thousand + 7 hundreds + 6 tens + 6 ones

122. _______________ 7 thousands + 2 hundreds + 8 tens + 6 ones

123. _______________ 1 thousand + 2 hundreds + 4 tens + 6 ones

124. _______________ 1 thousand + 2 hundreds + 6 tens + 7 ones

125. _______________ 9 thousands + 8 hundreds + 8 tens

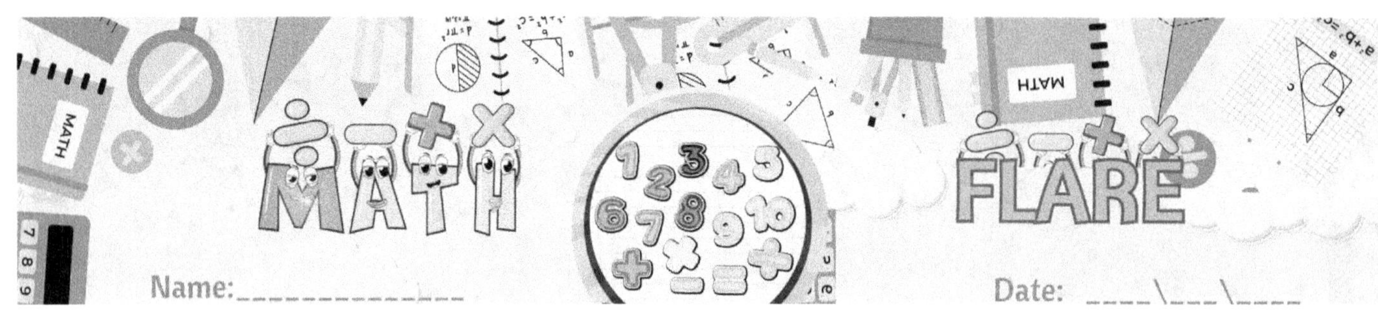

126. _______________ 7 thousands + 8 hundreds + 9 tens + 9 ones

127. _______________ 5 thousands + 9 hundreds + 2 tens + 2 ones

128. _______________ 9 thousands + 3 hundreds + 8 tens + 8 ones

129. _______________ 9 thousands + 5 hundreds + 4 tens

130. _______________ 5 hundreds + 6 tens + 5 ones

131. _______________ 6 thousands + 7 hundreds + 8 ones

132. _______________ 5 thousands + 6 tens + 9 ones

133. _______________ 7 thousands + 7 hundreds + 3 ones

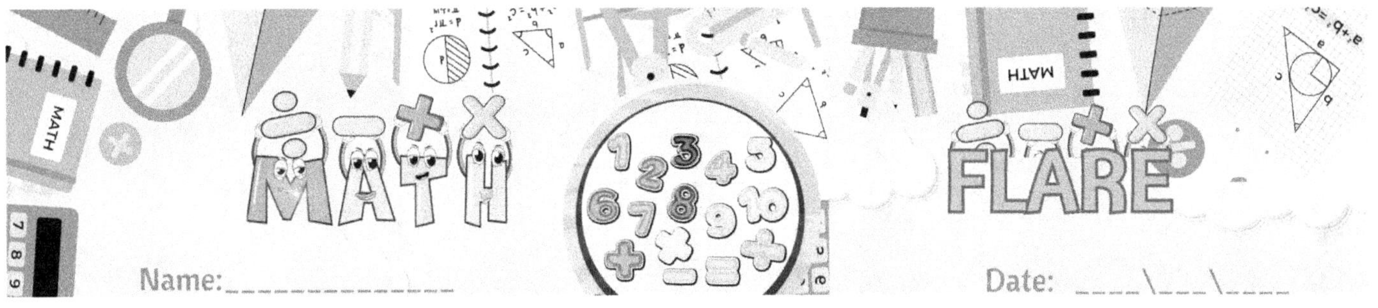

134. _______________ 8 thousands + 1 hundred + 3 tens + 4 ones

135. _______________ 4 thousands + 2 hundreds + 7 tens + 6 ones

136. _______________ 4 thousands + 8 hundreds + 3 tens + 2 ones

137. _______________ 8 thousands + 2 hundreds + 7 tens + 8 ones

138. _______________ 6 thousands + 2 hundreds + 6 tens + 5 ones

139. _______________ 6 thousands + 1 hundred + 3 tens + 1 one

140. _______________ 7 thousands + 5 hundreds + 3 tens + 3 ones

141. _______________ 4 thousands + 5 tens + 1 one

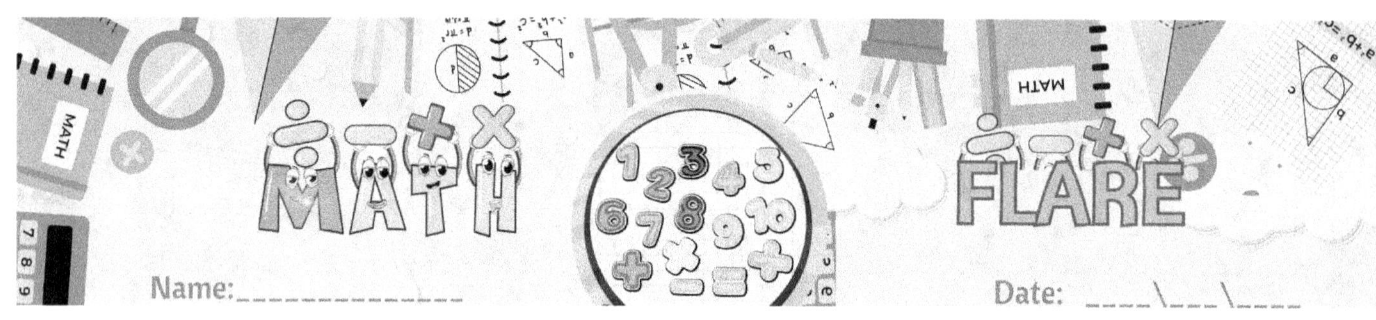

142. _______________ 2 thousands + 7 hundreds + 2 tens + 4 ones

143. _______________ 7 thousands + 4 hundreds + 4 tens + 1 one

144. _______________ 7 thousands + 2 hundreds + 1 ten + 5 ones

145. _______________ 7 thousands + 5 hundreds + 2 ones

146. _______________ 1 thousand + 8 hundreds + 9 tens + 7 ones

147. _______________ 1 thousand + 8 tens + 4 ones

148. _______________ 9 thousands + 2 hundreds + 3 tens + 4 ones

149. _______________ 6 thousands + 1 hundred + 3 tens + 6 ones

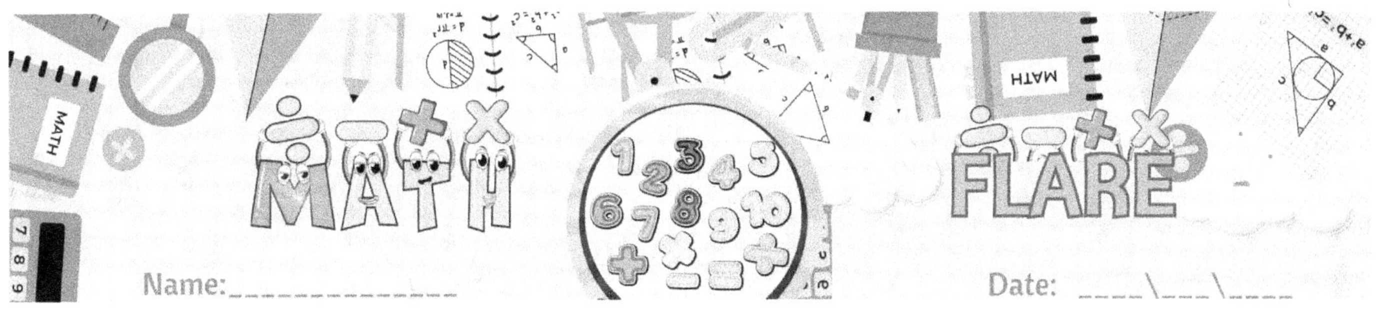

Name:________________   Date: ___________

150. _____________   3 hundreds + 2 tens + 4 ones

151. _____________   6 thousands + 5 hundreds + 8 tens + 8 ones

152. _____________   1 thousand + 6 hundreds + 5 tens + 5 ones

153. _____________   5 thousands + 4 hundreds + 3 tens + 6 ones

154. _____________   6 thousands + 3 hundreds + 7 tens + 3 ones

155. _____________   6 thousands + 4 hundreds + 2 tens + 9 ones

156. _____________   2 thousands + 4 hundreds + 3 tens + 9 ones

157. _____________   2 thousands + 8 hundreds + 1 ten + 7 ones

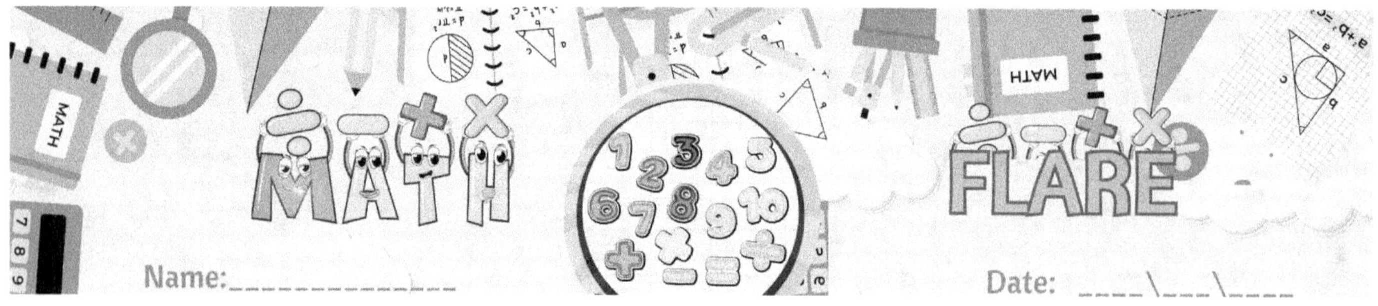

Place Value: Expanded Notation

Provide the expanded notation for each value.

158. 6,334 _______________

159. 535 _______________

160. 8,141 _______________

161. 5,984 _______________

162. 9,204 _______________

163. 1,314 _______________

164. 7,890 _______________

165. 5,833 _______________

166. 3,498 __________________

167. 6,197 __________________

168. 2,586 __________________

169. 3,534 __________________

170. 1,497 __________________

171. 4,697 __________________

172. 1,474 __________________

173. 1,277 __________________

174. 2,660 __________________

175. 2,404 __________________

176. 5,998 ___________________

177. 1,682 ___________________

178. 9,754 ___________________

179. 4,794 ___________________

180. 9,456 ___________________

181. 5,473 ___________________

182. 5,246 ___________________

183. 5,495 ___________________

184. 3,380 ___________________

185. 6,900 ___________________

186. 1,050 _______________

187. 2,639 _______________

188. 4,181 _______________

189. 5,606 _______________

190. 3,430 _______________

191. 8 _______________

192. 6,281 _______________

193. 5,316 _______________

194. 3,964 _______________

195. 7,186 _______________

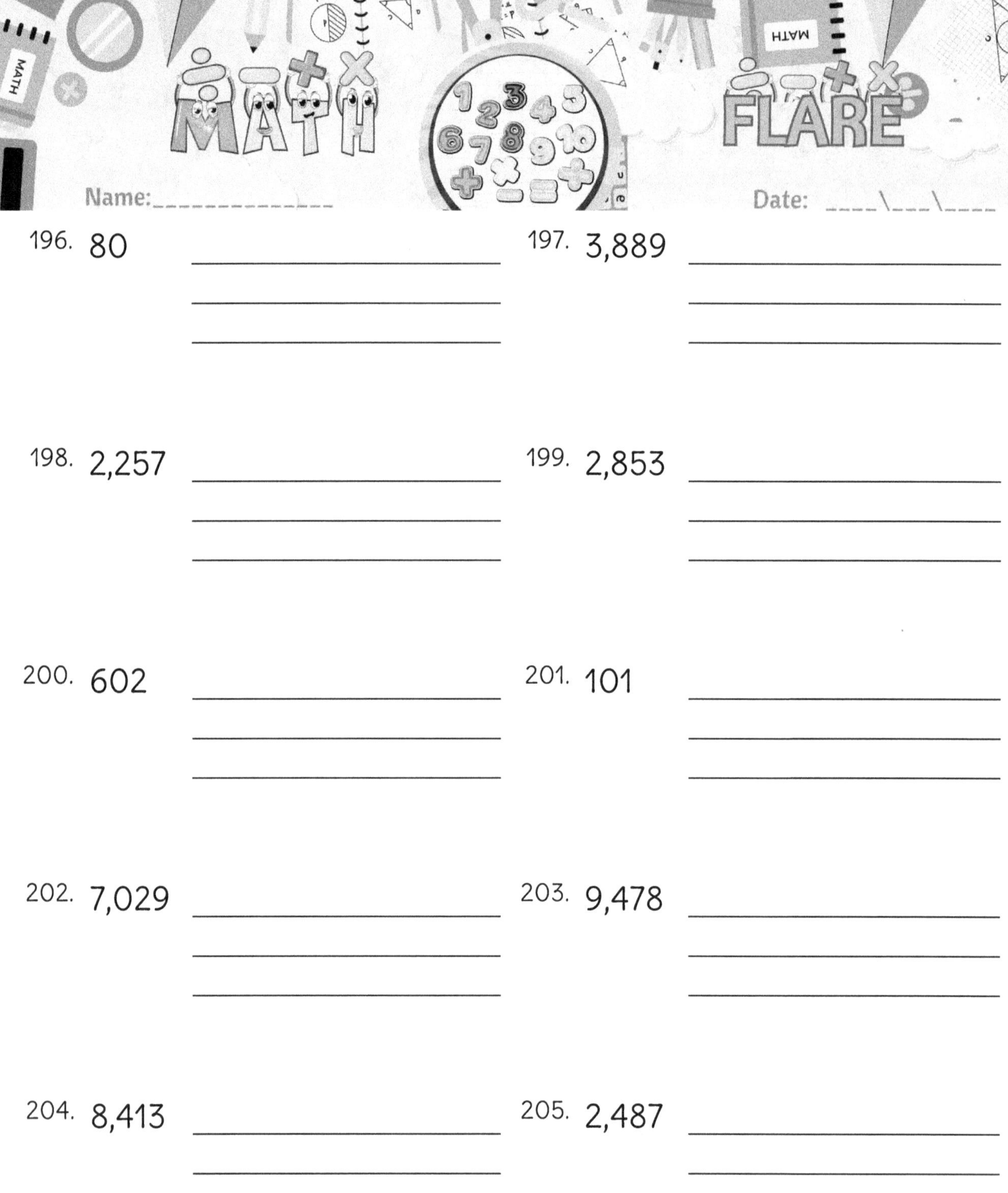

196. 80 ___________________

197. 3,889 ___________________

198. 2,257 ___________________

199. 2,853 ___________________

200. 602 ___________________

201. 101 ___________________

202. 7,029 ___________________

203. 9,478 ___________________

204. 8,413 ___________________

205. 2,487 ___________________

206. 1,605 __________________

207. 7,286 __________________

208. 6,768 __________________

209. 9,437 __________________

210. 423 __________________

211. 5,636 __________________

212. 1,242 __________________

213. 1,540 __________________

214. 1,078 __________________

215. 2,668 __________________

216. 739 ________________

217. 3,710 ________________

218. 7,934 ________________

219. 990 ________________

220. 4,783 ________________

221. 860 ________________

222. 2,017 ________________

223. 6,978 ________________

224. 104 ________________

225. 1,490 ________________

226. 8,415 ______________________

227. 6,157 ______________________

228. 7,312 ______________________

229. 2,324 ______________________

230. 2,110 ______________________

231. 9,424 ______________________

232. 6,902 ______________________

233. 4,193 ______________________

234. 9,356 ______________________

235. 8,444 ______________________

236. 5,767 _______________________

237. 7,081 _______________________

238. 894 _______________________

239. 5,296 _______________________

240. 3,763 _______________________

241. 5,870 _______________________

242. 4,743 _______________________

243. 5,184 _______________________

244. 7,793 _______________________

245. 8,766 _______________________

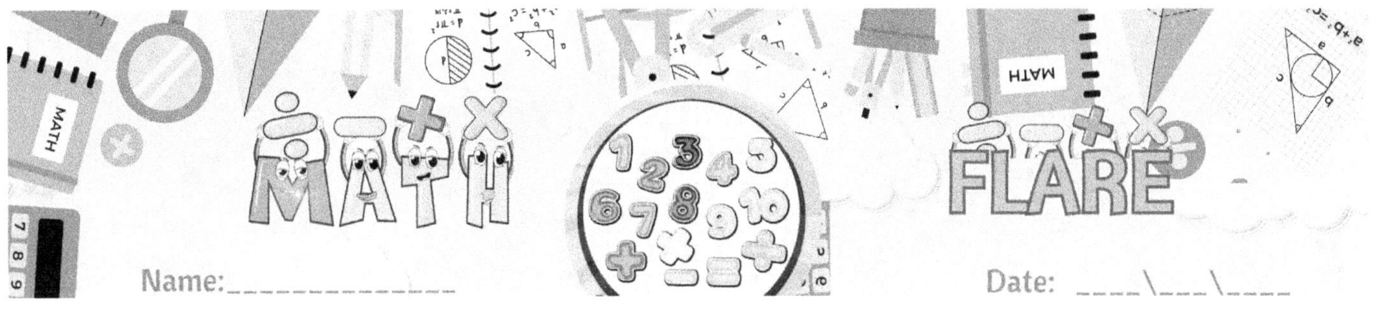

Place Value: Expanded Notation

Provide the expanded notation for each value.

246. _____________ 4,000 + 700 + 40 + 2

247. _____________ 4,000 + 200 + 30 + 9

248. _____________ 1,000 + 200 + 90 + 7

249. _____________ 6,000 + 400 + 40 + 8

250. _____________ 6,000 + 300 + 70

251. _____________ 5,000 + 900 + 50 + 4

252. _____________ 1,000 + 200 + 60 + 8

253. _____________ 8,000 + 60 + 8

254. _____________ 9,000 + 700 + 40 + 1

255. _____________ 8,000 + 80 + 3

256. ______________ $50 + 1$

257. ______________ $9,000 + 300 + 70 + 4$

258. ______________ $6,000 + 900 + 20 + 5$

259. ______________ $4,000 + 70 + 1$

260. ______________ $5,000 + 400 + 40 + 7$

261. ______________ $9,000 + 900 + 70 + 3$

262. ______________ $1,000 + 200 + 90 + 6$

263. ______________ $7,000 + 100 + 10 + 4$

264. ______________ $8,000 + 300 + 10 + 2$

265. ______________ $6,000 + 200 + 10 + 1$

266. ______________ $4,000 + 300 + 30 + 9$

267. ______________ $7,000 + 300 + 40 + 6$

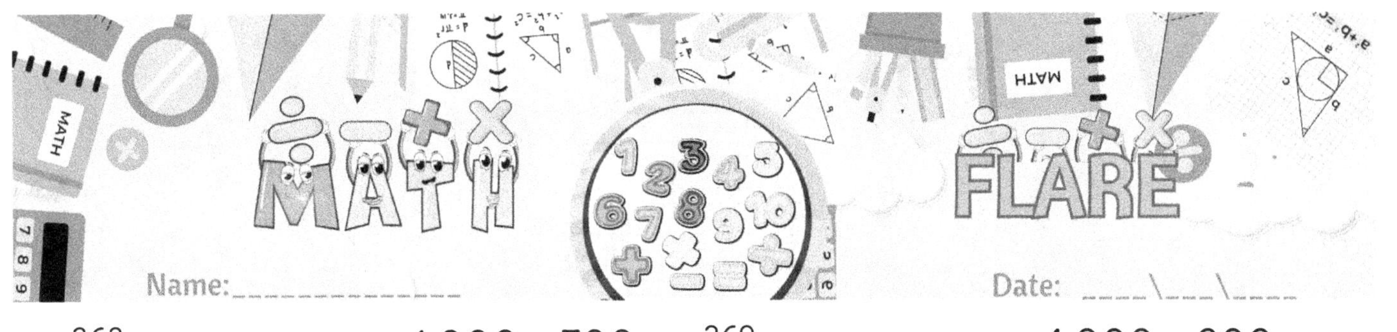

268. _____________ 1,000 + 700 + 20 + 1

269. _____________ 4,000 + 200 + 20 + 4

270. _____________ 4,000 + 900 + 70 + 1

271. _____________ 6,000 + 600 + 20 + 8

272. _____________ 7,000 + 40 + 1

273. _____________ 5,000 + 600 + 90 + 3

274. _____________ 1,000 + 20 + 1

275. _____________ 4,000 + 900 + 80 + 8

276. _____________ 7,000 + 200 + 70 + 3

277. _____________ 1,000 + 700 + 90 + 5

278. _____________ 2,000 + 300 + 10

279. _____________ 2,000 + 700 + 20 + 3

280. _____________ $3{,}000 + 600 + 70 + 4$

281. _____________ $1{,}000 + 900 + 10 + 9$

282. _____________ $6{,}000 + 10 + 6$

283. _____________ $9{,}000 + 20 + 4$

284. _____________ $5{,}000 + 900 + 50 + 3$

285. _____________ $6{,}000 + 100 + 50 + 4$

286. _____________ $8{,}000 + 100 + 50 + 7$

287. _____________ $8{,}000 + 800 + 30 + 2$

288. _____________ $4{,}000 + 400 + 50 + 1$

289. _____________ $1{,}000 + 200 + 70 + 4$

290. _____________ $8{,}000 + 300 + 90 + 3$

291. _____________ $6{,}000 + 300 + 90 + 2$

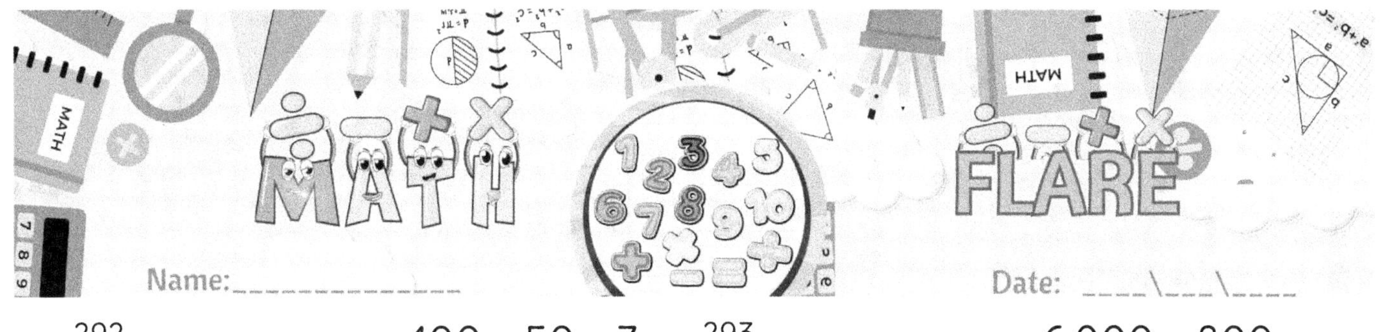

292. _____________   100 + 50 + 7

293. _____________   6,000 + 800 + 20 + 2

294. _____________   9,000 + 800 + 40 + 8

295. _____________   3,000 + 700 + 80 + 9

296. _____________   4,000 + 500 + 70 + 5

297. _____________   7,000 + 600 + 20 + 8

298. _____________   6,000 + 800 + 70 + 1

299. _____________   1,000 + 500 + 80 + 3

300. _____________   4,000 + 400 + 20 + 8

301. _____________   7,000 + 300 + 90 + 5

302. _____________   2,000 + 500 + 10 + 9

303. _____________   7,000 + 70 + 2

Name:_______________   Date: _______________

304. _______________ 1,000 + 400 + 70 + 7

305. _______________ 8,000 + 900 + 10 + 2

306. _______________ 5,000 + 500 + 70 + 4

307. _______________ 7,000 + 40 + 8

308. _______________ 4,000 + 700 + 50 + 4

309. _______________ 800 + 10 + 1

310. _______________ 8,000 + 200 + 50 + 5

311. _______________ 7,000 + 60 + 6

312. _______________ 4,000 + 200 + 3

313. _______________ 300 + 90 + 8

314. _______________ 3,000 + 500 + 30

315. _______________ 3,000 + 900 + 50 + 8

316. ____________ 2,000 + 200 + 70

317. ____________ 1,000 + 100 + 60 + 2

318. ____________ 2,000 + 100 + 50 + 9

319. ____________ 8,000 + 50 + 3

320. ____________ 5,000 + 500 + 6

321. ____________ 2,000 + 800 + 90 + 6

322. ____________ 400 + 40 + 8

323. ____________ 5,000 + 800 + 20 + 9

324. ____________ 8,000 + 500 + 70 + 8

325. ____________ 6,000 + 400 + 70 + 2

326. ____________ 200 + 20

327. ____________ 5,000 + 800 + 40 + 4

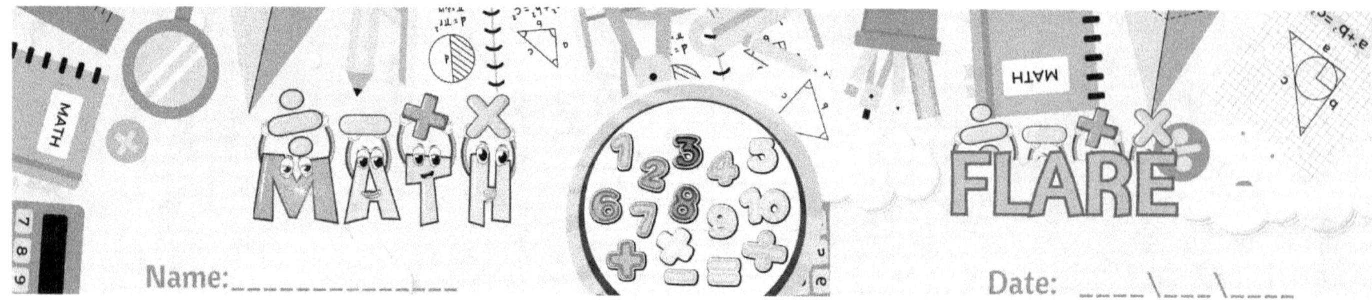

Place Value: Expanded Notation

Provide the expanded notation for each value.

328. 7,231 _______________________

329. 414 _______________________

330. 9,644 _______________________

331. 4,923 _______________________

332. 728 _______________________

333. 8,294 _______________________

334. 6,278 _______________________

335. 9,398 _______________________

336. 8,943 _______________________

337. 7,548 _______________________

338. 6,211 _______________________
____

339. 7,241 _______________________
____

340. 2,584 _______________________
____

341. 1,785 _______________________
____

342. 9,696 _______________________
____

343. 464 _______________________
____

344. 139 _______________________
____

345. 9,325 _______________________
____

346. 5,953 _______________________
____

347. 6,425 _______________________
____

348. 6,319 _______________________
____

349. 9,830 _______________________
____

350. 2,306 ____________________
____

351. 6,467 ____________________
____

352. 4,713 ____________________
____

353. 3,529 ____________________
____

354. 8,921 ____________________
____

355. 4,500 ____________________
____

356. 2,073 ____________________
____

357. 1,244 ____________________
____

358. 2,898 ____________________
____

359. 3,270 ____________________
____

360. 8,693 ____________________
____

361. 9,729 ____________________
____

362. 9,816 ________________________

363. 4,341 ________________________

364. 1,166 ________________________

365. 3,332 ________________________

366. 6,339 ________________________

367. 5,908 ________________________

368. 4,118 ________________________

369. 4,131 ________________________

370. 5,015 ________________________

371. 4,721 ________________________

372. 4,949 ________________________

373. 4,917 ________________________

374. 5,470 __________________

375. 3,722 __________________

376. 3,199 __________________

377. 9,983 __________________

378. 5,691 __________________

379. 9,252 __________________

380. 519 __________________

381. 3,794 __________________

382. 9,524 __________________

383. 7,401 __________________

384. 8,107 __________________

385. 3,178 __________________

386. 211 _______________________

387. 7,197 _______________________

388. 9,372 _______________________

389. 1,779 _______________________

390. 7,326 _______________________

391. 7,699 _______________________

392. 4,651 _______________________

393. 2,942 _______________________

394. 8,547 _______________________

395. 2,854 _______________________

396. 1,968 _______________________

397. 5,355 _______________________

398. 9,297 ________________

399. 6,806 ________________

400. 2,987 ________________

401. 47 ________________

402. 2,308 ________________

403. 2,190 ________________

404. 4,816 ________________

405. 7,584 ________________

406. 1,519 ________________

407. 9,795 ________________

408. 8,058 ________________

409. 5,200 ________________

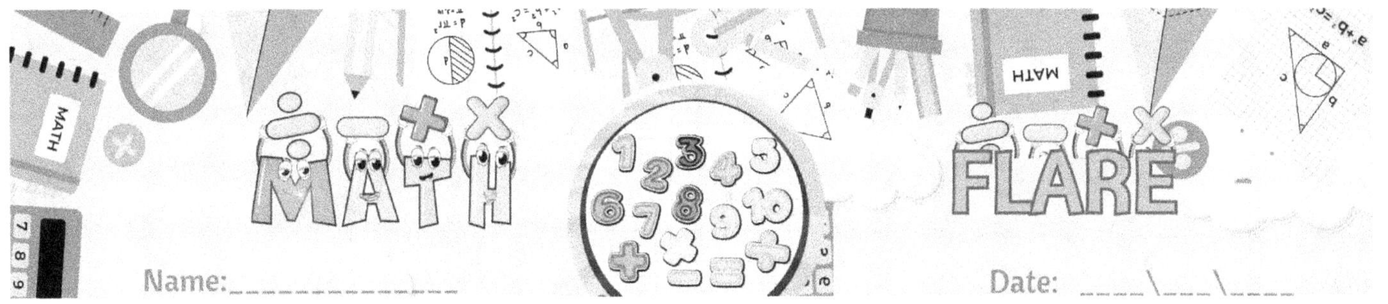

Name:____________________   Date: _________

Place Value: Expanded Notation

Provide the expanded notation for each value.

410. ______________ one thousand three hundred two

411. ______________ two thousand eighty-nine

412. ______________ five thousand five hundred fifty-two

413. ______________ three thousand six hundred forty-five

414. ______________ two thousand seven hundred fifty-two

415. ______________ four thousand nine hundred

416. _______________ two hundred six

417. _______________ two thousand four hundred sixteen

418. _______________ six thousand two hundred thirty-four

419. _______________ seven thousand nine hundred eighty-seven

420. _______________ three thousand one hundred twenty-two

421. _______________ nine thousand one hundred forty

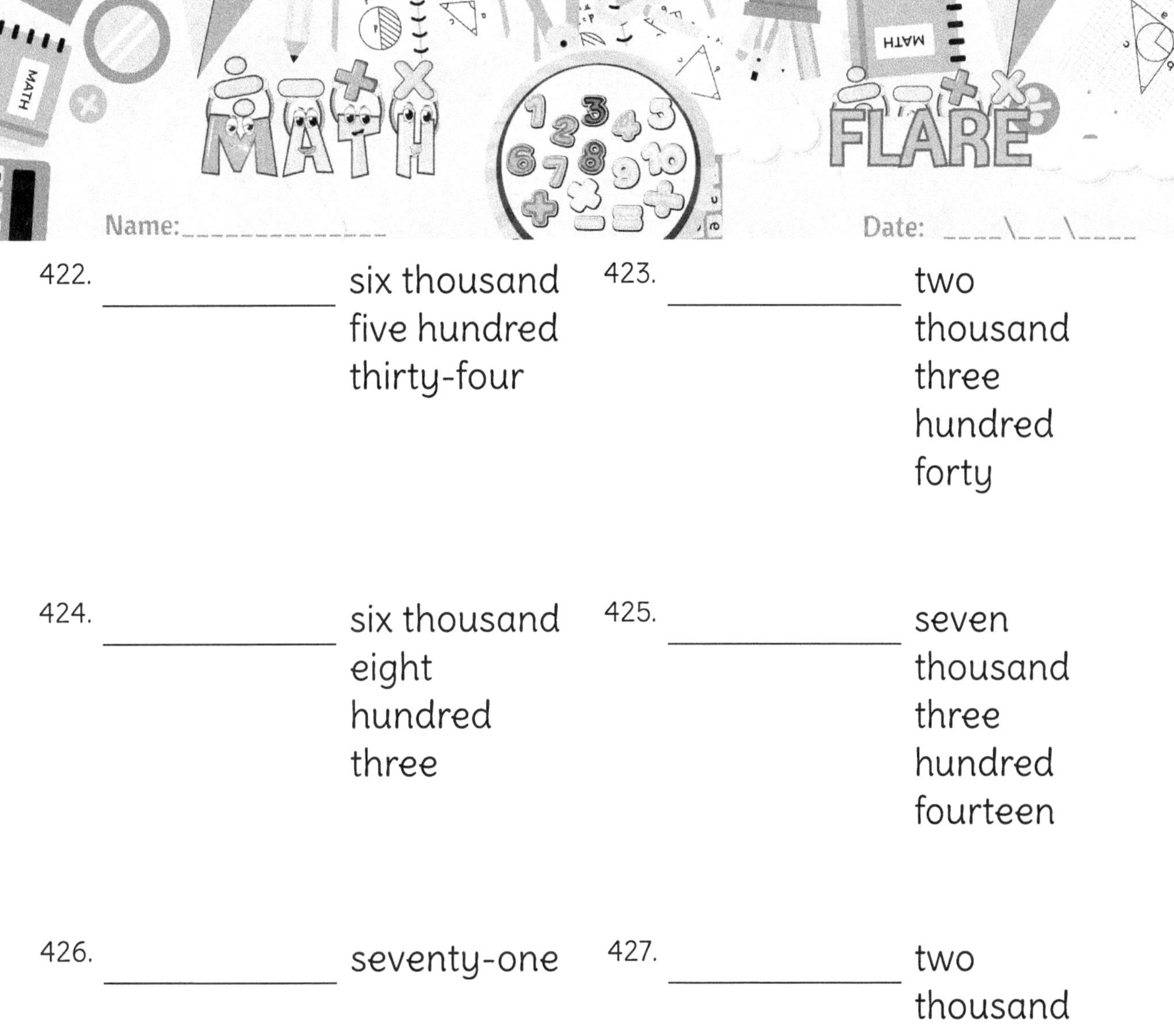

422. ________________ six thousand five hundred thirty-four

423. ________________ two thousand three hundred forty

424. ________________ six thousand eight hundred three

425. ________________ seven thousand three hundred fourteen

426. ________________ seventy-one

427. ________________ two thousand nine

428. _________________ six thousand three hundred sixty-nine

429. _________________ two thousand six hundred seventeen

430. _________________ one thousand seven hundred fifty-five

431. _________________ seven thousand eight hundred forty-three

432. _________________ six hundred eighty-seven

433. _________________ eight thousand eight hundred eighty-four

434. ______________ six thousand two hundred sixty-six

435. ______________ four hundred seventy-four

436. ______________ one thousand four hundred eighty-seven

437. ______________ seven thousand three hundred thirty-five

438. ______________ two thousand five hundred eighty-six

439. ______________ five hundred twenty-four

440. _______________ one thousand six hundred sixty

441. _______________ four hundred fifteen

442. _______________ nine thousand one hundred thirty-eight

443. _______________ four thousand one hundred seventy-three

444. _______________ four hundred seventy-nine

445. _______________ five thousand two hundred thirty-nine

446. ______________ two thousand one hundred forty-eight

447. ______________ one thousand eight

448. ______________ one hundred ninety-one

449. ______________ three thousand six hundred forty-eight

450. ______________ two thousand six hundred forty-nine

451. ______________ nine thousand five hundred fifty -one

452. _______________ nine thousand one hundred twenty-one

453. _______________ one thousand three hundred eleven

454. _______________ three thousand six hundred eighty-five

455. _______________ three thousand eight hundred forty-six

456. _______________ three thousand five hundred twelve

457. _______________ nine thousand nine hundred sixty-seven

458. __________________ five thousand three hundred eighty-six

459. __________________ seven thousand five hundred one

460. __________________ seven thousand five hundred fourteen

461. __________________ nine thousand five hundred nine

462. __________________ three thousand four hundred twenty-eight

463. __________________ five thousand four hundred forty-three

464. _______________ three thousand four hundred forty-six

465. _______________ three thousand four hundred fifty-eight

466. _______________ one thousand four hundred three

467. _______________ six thousand six hundred sixty-eight

468. _______________ seven thousand three hundred seventy-eight

469. _______________ two thousand two hundred eighty

470. ______________ three thousand four hundred fourteen

471. ______________ two thousand eight hundred seventy

472. ______________ nine thousand eight hundred twenty-nine

473. ______________ five thousand seven hundred eleven

474. ______________ six thousand three hundred twenty-eight

475. ______________ two thousand seven hundred eight

476. _______________ three

477. _______________ two thousand three hundred sixty -two

478. _______________ one thousand eight hundred sixty -two

479. _______________ one thousand five hundred sixty-five

480. _______________ five thousand one hundred sixty-seven

481. _______________ nine thousand sixty-three

482. ______________ one thousand eight hundred nineteen

483. ______________ two thousand seven hundred twenty-two

484. ______________ two thousand two hundred three

485. ______________ eight thousand seven hundred twenty-one

486. ______________ nine thousand three hundred seventy-five

487. ______________ five thousand two hundred

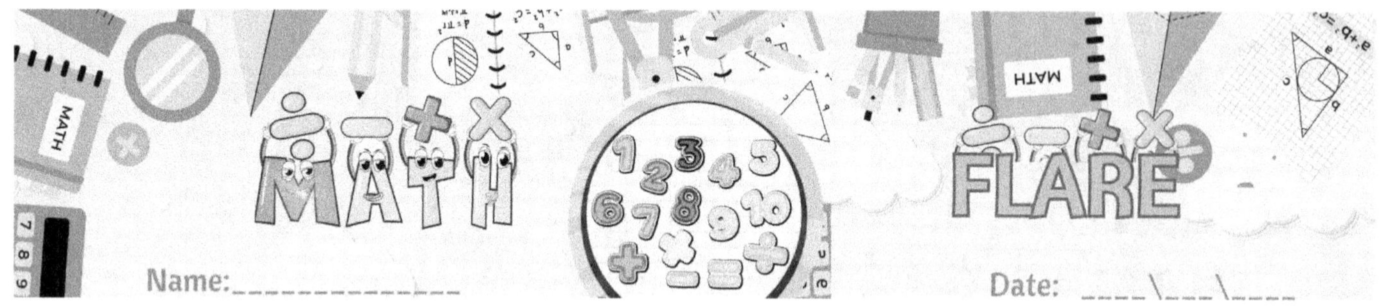

Name:________________   Date: ____________

Place Value: Expanded Notation

Provide the expanded notation for each value.

488. 993 _______________________

____

489. 315 _______________________

____

490. 687 _______________________

____

491. 520 _______________________

____

492. 218 _______________________

____

493. 528 _______________________

____

494. 176 _______________________

____

495. 476 _______________________

____

496. 732 _______________________

____

497. 226 _______________________

____

498. 140 _______________________

499. 890 _______________________

500. 623 _______________________

501. 855 _______________________

502. 880 _______________________

503. 597 _______________________

504. 433 _______________________

505. 977 _______________________

506. 785 _______________________

507. 541 _______________________

508. 15 _______________________

509. 760 _______________________

510. 842 ______________________

511. 798 ______________________

512. 261 ______________________

513. 247 ______________________

514. 459 ______________________

515. 499 ______________________

516. 778 ______________________

517. 689 ______________________

518. 428 ______________________

519. 612 ______________________

520. 271 ______________________

521. 688 ______________________

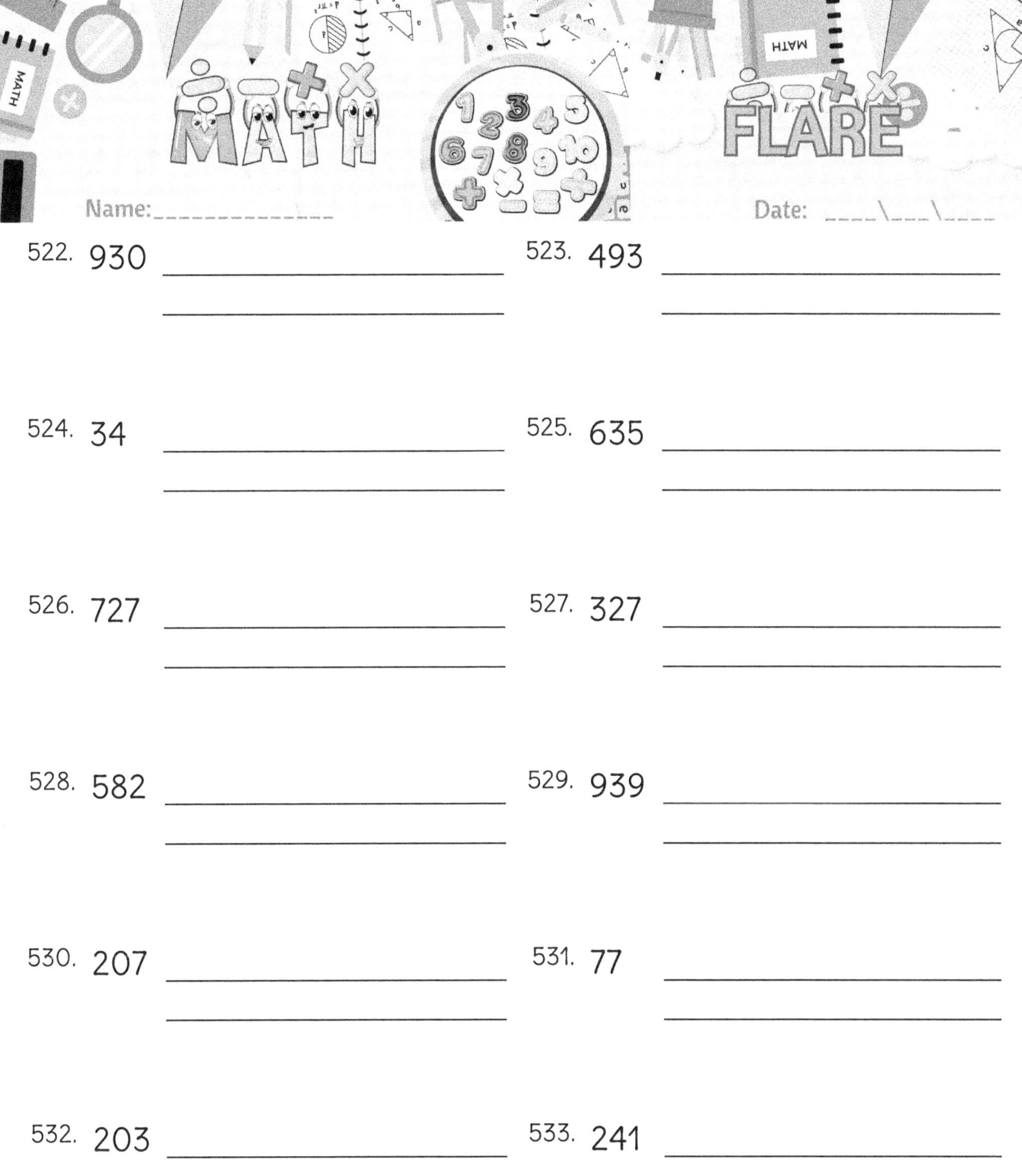

522. 930 ________________________

523. 493 ________________________

524. 34 ________________________

525. 635 ________________________

526. 727 ________________________

527. 327 ________________________

528. 582 ________________________

529. 939 ________________________

530. 207 ________________________

531. 77 ________________________

532. 203 ________________________

533. 241 ________________________

534. 827 ___________________

535. 549 ___________________

536. 789 ___________________

537. 791 ___________________

538. 497 ___________________

539. 510 ___________________

540. 845 ___________________

541. 43 ___________________

542. 234 ___________________

543. 471 ___________________

544. 888 ___________________

545. 259 ___________________

ANSWERS

Page 1:   Place Value

1. 3 hundreds

2. 1 thousand

3. 8 hundreds

4. 2 thousands

5. 2 tens

6. 6 ones

7. 9 hundreds

8. 2 ones

9. 1 one

10. 3 tens

11. 1 hundred

12. 0 hundreds

13. 0 ones

14. 8 thousands

15. 8 ones

16. 8 hundreds

17. 1 thousand

18. 1 ten

19. 2 ones

20. 4 tens

21. 5 hundreds

22. 9 hundreds

23. 2 tens

24. 2 ones

25. 3 ones

26. 9 hundreds

27. 5 tens

28. 5 thousands

29. 0 tens

30. 9 thousands

31. 4 thousands

32. 7 thousands

33. 3 thousands

34. 4 hundreds

35. 0 tens

36. 7 tens

37. 3 tens

38. 2 ones

39. 6 tens

40. 3 tens

41. 3 ones

42. 3 ones

43. 9 hundreds

44. 7 hundreds

45. 1 ten

46. 6 ones

47. 4 tens

48. 3 tens

49. 5 hundreds

50. 6 tens

51. 5 hundreds

52. 5 thousands

53. 1 one

54. 5 hundreds

55. 5 tens

56. 4 hundreds

57. 6 tens

58. 3 ones   59. 6 thousands   60. 7 ones

61. 6 ones   62. 5 ones   63. 3 thousands

64. 3 hundreds   65. 7 ones   66. 5 hundreds

67. 2 thousands   68. 6 thousands   69. 2 hundreds

70. 1 hundred   71. 2 hundreds   72. 2 ones

73. 5 thousands   74. 2 ones   75. 8 tens

76. 4 hundreds   77. 0 hundreds   78. 5 tens

Page 6:   Place Value: Expanded Notation

79. 6,273   80. 7,990   81. 8,516   82. 2,362   83. 7,945

84. 773   85. 2,852   86. 1,834   87. 8,095   88. 6,478

89. 2,016   90. 1,536   91. 285   92. 7,053   93. 173

94. 7,211   95. 3,205   96. 1,945   97. 8,987   98. 4,542

99. 4,961   100. 8,138   101. 3,716   102. 3,684   103. 4,083

104. 1,681   105. 4,640   106. 5,318   107. 7,782   108. 5,372

109. 9,035   110. 4,070   111. 4,320   112. 2,782   113. 5,157

114. 9,088   115. 7,976   116. 7,068   117. 1,622   118. 2,400

119. 2,888   120. 9,524   121. 1,766   122. 7,286   123. 1,246

124. 1,267   125. 9,880   126. 7,899   127. 5,922   128. 9,388

129. 9,540   130. 565   131. 6,708   132. 5,069   133. 7,703

134. 8,134   135. 4,276   136. 4,832   137. 8,278   138. 6,265

139. 6,131   140. 7,533   141. 4,051   142. 2,724   143. 7,441

144. 7,215   145. 7,502   146. 1,897   147. 1,084   148. 9,234

149. 6,136   150. 324   151. 6,588   152. 1,655   153. 5,436

154. 6,373   155. 6,429   156. 2,439   157. 2,817

Page 16:   Place Value: Expanded Notation

158. 6 thousands + 3 hundreds + 3 tens + 4 ones

159. 5 hundreds + 3 tens + 5 ones

160. 8 thousands + 1 hundred + 4 tens + 1 one

161. 5 thousands + 9 hundreds + 8 tens + 4 ones

162. 9 thousands + 2 hundreds + 4 ones

163. 1 thousand + 3 hundreds + 1 ten + 4 ones

164. 7 thousands + 8 hundreds + 9 tens

165. 5 thousands + 8 hundreds + 3 tens + 3 ones

166. 3 thousands + 4 hundreds + 9 tens + 8 ones

167. 6 thousands + 1 hundred + 9 tens + 7 ones

168. 2 thousands + 5 hundreds + 8 tens + 6 ones

169. 3 thousands + 5 hundreds + 3 tens + 4 ones

170. 1 thousand + 4 hundreds + 9 tens + 7 ones

171. 4 thousands + 6 hundreds + 9 tens + 7 ones

172. 1 thousand + 4 hundreds + 7 tens + 4 ones

173. 1 thousand + 2 hundreds + 7 tens + 7 ones

174. 2 thousands + 6 hundreds + 6 tens

175. 2 thousands + 4 hundreds + 4 ones

176. 5 thousands + 9 hundreds + 9 tens + 8 ones

177. 1 thousand + 6 hundreds + 8 tens + 2 ones

178. 9 thousands + 7 hundreds + 5 tens + 4 ones

179. 4 thousands + 7 hundreds + 9 tens + 4 ones

180. 9 thousands + 4 hundreds + 5 tens + 6 ones

181. 5 thousands + 4 hundreds + 7 tens + 3 ones

182. 5 thousands + 2 hundreds + 4 tens + 6 ones

183. 5 thousands + 4 hundreds + 9 tens + 5 ones

184. 3 thousands + 3 hundreds + 8 tens

185. 6 thousands + 9 hundreds

186. 1 thousand + 5 tens

187. 2 thousands + 6 hundreds + 3 tens + 9 ones

188. 4 thousands + 1 hundred + 8 tens + 1 one

189. 5 thousands + 6 hundreds + 6 ones

190. 3 thousands + 4 hundreds + 3 tens

191. 8 ones

192. 6 thousands + 2 hundreds + 8 tens + 1 one

193. 5 thousands + 3 hundreds + 1 ten + 6 ones

194. 3 thousands + 9 hundreds + 6 tens + 4 ones

195. 7 thousands + 1 hundred + 8 tens + 6 ones

196. 8 tens

197. 3 thousands + 8 hundreds + 8 tens + 9 ones

198. 2 thousands + 2 hundreds + 5 tens + 7 ones

199. 2 thousands + 8 hundreds + 5 tens + 3 ones

200. 6 hundreds + 2 ones

201. 1 hundred + 1 one

202. 7 thousands + 2 tens + 9 ones

203. 9 thousands + 4 hundreds + 7 tens + 8 ones

204. 8 thousands + 4 hundreds + 1 ten + 3 ones

205. 2 thousands + 4 hundreds + 8 tens + 7 ones

206. 1 thousand + 6 hundreds + 5 ones

207. 7 thousands + 2 hundreds + 8 tens + 6 ones

208. 6 thousands + 7 hundreds + 6 tens + 8 ones

209. 9 thousands + 4 hundreds + 3 tens + 7 ones

210. 4 hundreds + 2 tens + 3 ones

211. 5 thousands + 6 hundreds + 3 tens + 6 ones

212. 1 thousand + 2 hundreds + 4 tens + 2 ones

213. 1 thousand + 5 hundreds + 4 tens

214. 1 thousand + 7 tens + 8 ones

215. 2 thousands + 6 hundreds + 6 tens + 8 ones

216. 7 hundreds + 3 tens + 9 ones

217. 3 thousands + 7 hundreds + 1 ten

218. 7 thousands + 9 hundreds + 3 tens + 4 ones

219. 9 hundreds + 9 tens

220. 4 thousands + 7 hundreds + 8 tens + 3 ones

221. 8 hundreds + 6 tens

222. 2 thousands + 1 ten + 7 ones

223. 6 thousands + 9 hundreds + 7 tens + 8 ones

224. 1 hundred + 4 ones

225. 1 thousand + 4 hundreds + 9 tens

226. 8 thousands + 4 hundreds + 1 ten + 5 ones

227. 6 thousands + 1 hundred + 5 tens + 7 ones

228. 7 thousands + 3 hundreds + 1 ten + 2 ones

229. 2 thousands + 3 hundreds + 2 tens + 4 ones

230. 2 thousands + 1 hundred + 1 ten

231. 9 thousands + 4 hundreds + 2 tens + 4 ones

232. 6 thousands + 9 hundreds + 2 ones

233. 4 thousands + 1 hundred + 9 tens + 3 ones

234. 9 thousands + 3 hundreds + 5 tens + 6 ones

235. 8 thousands + 4 hundreds + 4 tens + 4 ones

236. 5 thousands + 7 hundreds + 6 tens + 7 ones

237. 7 thousands + 8 tens + 1 one

238. 8 hundreds + 9 tens + 4 ones

239. 5 thousands + 2 hundreds + 9 tens + 6 ones

240. 3 thousands + 7 hundreds + 6 tens + 3 ones

241. 5 thousands + 8 hundreds + 7 tens

242. 4 thousands + 7 hundreds + 4 tens + 3 ones

243. 5 thousands + 1 hundred + 8 tens + 4 ones

244. 7 thousands + 7 hundreds + 9 tens + 3 ones

245. 8 thousands + 7 hundreds + 6 tens + 6 ones

Page 25: Place Value: Expanded Notation

246. 4,742	247. 4,239	248. 1,297	249. 6,448	250. 6,370
251. 5,954	252. 1,268	253. 8,068	254. 9,741	255. 8,083
256. 51	257. 9,374	258. 6,925	259. 4,071	260. 5,447
261. 9,973	262. 1,296	263. 7,114	264. 8,312	265. 6,211
266. 4,339	267. 7,346	268. 1,721	269. 4,224	270. 4,971
271. 6,628	272. 7,041	273. 5,693	274. 1,021	275. 4,988
276. 7,273	277. 1,795	278. 2,310	279. 2,723	280. 3,674
281. 1,919	282. 6,016	283. 9,024	284. 5,953	285. 6,154
286. 8,157	287. 8,832	288. 4,451	289. 1,274	290. 8,393
291. 6,392	292. 157	293. 6,822	294. 9,848	295. 3,789
296. 4,575	297. 7,628	298. 6,871	299. 1,583	300. 4,428
301. 7,395	302. 2,519	303. 7,072	304. 1,477	305. 8,912

306. 5,574   307. 7,048   308. 4,754   309. 811   310. 8,255

311. 7,066   312. 4,203   313. 398   314. 3,530   315. 3,958

316. 2,270   317. 1,162   318. 2,159   319. 8,053   320. 5,506

321. 2,896   322. 448   323. 5,829   324. 8,578   325. 6,472

326. 220   327. 5,844

Page 32:   Place Value: Expanded Notation

328. 7,000 + 200 + 30 + 1

329. 400 + 10 + 4

330. 9,000 + 600 + 40 + 4

331. 4,000 + 900 + 20 + 3

332. 700 + 20 + 8

333. 8,000 + 200 + 90 + 4

334. 6,000 + 200 + 70 + 8

335. 9,000 + 300 + 90 + 8

336. 8,000 + 900 + 40 + 3

337. 7,000 + 500 + 40 + 8

338. 6,000 + 200 + 10 + 1

339. 7,000 + 200 + 40 + 1

340. 2,000 + 500 + 80 + 4

341. 1,000 + 700 + 80 + 5

342. 9,000 + 600 + 90 + 6

343. 400 + 60 + 4

344. 100 + 30 + 9

345. 9,000 + 300 + 20 + 5

346. 5,000 + 900 + 50 + 3

347. 6,000 + 400 + 20 + 5

348. 6,000 + 300 + 10 + 9

349. 9,000 + 800 + 30

350. 2,000 + 300 + 6

351. 6,000 + 400 + 60 + 7

352. 4,000 + 700 + 10 + 3

353. 3,000 + 500 + 20 + 9

354. 8,000 + 900 + 20 + 1

355. 4,000 + 500

356. 2,000 + 70 + 3

357. 1,000 + 200 + 40 + 4

358. 2,000 + 800 + 90 + 8

359. 3,000 + 200 + 70

360. 8,000 + 600 + 90 + 3

361. 9,000 + 700 + 20 + 9

362. 9,000 + 800 + 10 + 6

363. 4,000 + 300 + 40 + 1

364. 1,000 + 100 + 60 + 6

365. 3,000 + 300 + 30 + 2

366. 6,000 + 300 + 30 + 9

367. 5,000 + 900 + 8

368. 4,000 + 100 + 10 + 8

369. 4,000 + 100 + 30 + 1

370. 5,000 + 10 + 5

371. 4,000 + 700 + 20 + 1

372. 4,000 + 900 + 40 + 9

373. 4,000 + 900 + 10 + 7

374. 5,000 + 400 + 70

375. 3,000 + 700 + 20 + 2

376. 3,000 + 100 + 90 + 9

377. 9,000 + 900 + 80 + 3

378. 5,000 + 600 + 90 + 1

379. 9,000 + 200 + 50 + 2

380. 500 + 10 + 9

381. 3,000 + 700 + 90 + 4

382. 9,000 + 500 + 20 + 4

383. 7,000 + 400 + 1

384. 8,000 + 100 + 7

385. 3,000 + 100 + 70 + 8

386. 200 + 10 + 1

387. 7,000 + 100 + 90 + 7

388. 9,000 + 300 + 70 + 2

389. 1,000 + 700 + 70 + 9

390. 7,000 + 300 + 20 + 6

391. 7,000 + 600 + 90 + 9

392. 4,000 + 600 + 50 + 1

393. 2,000 + 900 + 40 + 2

394. 8,000 + 500 + 40 + 7

395. 2,000 + 800 + 50 + 4

396. 1,000 + 900 + 60 + 8

397. 5,000 + 300 + 50 + 5

398. 9,000 + 200 + 90 + 7

399. 6,000 + 800 + 6

400. 2,000 + 900 + 80 + 7   401. 40 + 7

402. 2,000 + 300 + 8   403. 2,000 + 100 + 90

404. 4,000 + 800 + 10 + 6   405. 7,000 + 500 + 80 + 4

406. 1,000 + 500 + 10 + 9   407. 9,000 + 700 + 90 + 5

408. 8,000 + 50 + 8   409. 5,000 + 200

Page 39:   Place Value: Expanded Notation

410. 1,302	411. 2,089	412. 5,552	413. 3,645	414. 2,752
415. 4,900	416. 206	417. 2,416	418. 6,234	419. 7,987
420. 3,122	421. 9,140	422. 6,534	423. 2,340	424. 6,803
425. 7,314	426. 71	427. 2,009	428. 6,369	429. 2,617
430. 1,755	431. 7,843	432. 687	433. 8,884	434. 6,266
435. 474	436. 1,487	437. 7,335	438. 2,586	439. 524
440. 1,660	441. 415	442. 9,138	443. 4,173	444. 479
445. 5,239	446. 2,148	447. 1,008	448. 191	449. 3,648
450. 2,649	451. 9,551	452. 9,121	453. 1,311	454. 3,685
455. 3,846	456. 3,512	457. 9,967	458. 5,386	459. 7,501
460. 7,514	461. 9,509	462. 3,428	463. 5,443	464. 3,446
465. 3,458	466. 1,403	467. 6,668	468. 7,378	469. 2,280
470. 3,414	471. 2,870	472. 9,829	473. 5,711	474. 6,328
475. 2,708	476. 3	477. 2,362	478. 1,862	479. 1,565
480. 5,167	481. 9,063	482. 1,819	483. 2,722	484. 2,203

485. 8,721   486. 9,375   487. 5,200

Page 52:   Place Value: Expanded Notation

488. nine hundred ninety-three

489. three hundred fifteen

490. six hundred eighty-seven

491. five hundred twenty

492. two hundred eighteen

493. five hundred twenty-eight

494. one hundred seventy-six

495. four hundred seventy-six

496. seven hundred thirty-two

497. two hundred twenty-six

498. one hundred forty

499. eight hundred ninety

500. six hundred twenty-three

501. eight hundred fifty-five

502. eight hundred eighty

503. five hundred ninety-seven

504. four hundred thirty-three

505. nine hundred seventy-seven

506. seven hundred eighty-five

507. five hundred forty-one

508. fifteen

509. seven hundred sixty

510. eight hundred forty-two

511. seven hundred ninety-eight

512. two hundred sixty-one

513. two hundred forty-seven

514. four hundred fifty-nine

515. four hundred ninety-nine

516. seven hundred seventy-eight

517. six hundred eighty-nine

518. four hundred twenty-eight

519. six hundred twelve

520. two hundred seventy-one

521. six hundred eighty-eight

522. nine hundred thirty

523. four hundred ninety-three

524. thirty-four

525. six hundred thirty-five

526. seven hundred twenty-seven

527. three hundred twenty-seven

528. five hundred eighty-two

529. nine hundred thirty-nine

530. two hundred seven

531. seventy-seven

532. two hundred three

533. two hundred forty-one

534. eight hundred twenty-seven

535. five hundred forty-nine

536. seven hundred eighty-nine

537. seven hundred ninety-one

538. four hundred ninety-seven

539. five hundred ten

540. eight hundred forty-five

541. forty-three

542. two hundred thirty-four

543. four hundred seventy-one

544. eight hundred eighty-eight

545. two hundred fifty-nine

9 798869 180827